INTRODUCTION

NOTES FOR PARENTS AND TEACHERS

The Programmes of Study in Science have been divided into three areas which are contained in the tests in this book. The tests contain much of the work to be covered by the end of a child's primary career.

The material can be used to highlight the areas with which the child is unfamiliar or which need explanation and further practice.

This ma[...] also be of use in preparing the chil[...]sts.

There i[...]

Many c[...]ests are explained in the glossary. Explanations are kept simple.

GLOSSARY

Abdomen: Back part of insect and without limbs. In humans the lower part of the body containing digestive and other organs.

Absorbent: The ability to suck up something e.g. as tissue paper sucks up water.

Air Pressure: The weight of air pushing down on the earth. Measured with a barometer.

Air Resistance: Friction between air and a moving object.

Amphibian: Creature able to live on land and in water.

Arteries: Tubes carrying blood away from the heart.

Asbestos: A fireproof material, the dust of which can damage our lungs.

Asteroid: A minor or very small planet.

Atmosphere: Mass of gases surrounding the earth.

Brine: Water containing a lot of salt.

Bronze: A metal made from a mixture of copper and tin.

Canines: Sharp-pointed teeth between incisors and molars.

Capillaries: Very thin tubes connecting arteries with veins.

Carbohydrate: A substance which contains sugars and starches.

Carbon Dioxide: A gas made up of one part carbon to two parts of oxygen.

Cell: The unit of which all living things are made.

Chlorophyll: A chemical contained in green leaves. It gives the leaves their colour.

Circuit: A continuous loop around which an electric current will flow.

Cold Blooded: A creature whose blood temperature changes to match that of its surroundings.

Comets: Lumps of rock and ice which orbit the sun.

Condensation: The process of a gas changing into a liquid e.g. when steam hits a cold surface.

Conductor: Material through which heat or electricity passes.

Diaphragm: A muscle which assists breathing.

Echo: Sound waves which are bounced back.

Effort: (see load) part of a lever system. The effort is the pressure or work that is applied to move the load.

Energy: The ability to do work.

Evaporation: The process of a liquid changing into a gas e.g. wet roads drying on a sunny day.

Fair Test: Only one thing, feature, condition etc must be changed. Everything else must remain constant or the same.

Fat: Oily substance found in animals.

Fertilisation: The meeting of male and female cells. In plants the transfer of pollen.

Fertiliser: Substance added to growing material in order to increase the growth of a plant and/or its fruit.

Fibre: Roughage which helps digestion.

Fibre-glass: Glass fibres used for insulation etc.

Fin: An organ by which a fish etc steers and swims.

Flexible: Something that is easily bent.

Force: A push or a pull causing things to move or change shape or direction.

Friction: A force that slows things down or stops them moving.

Fruit: The part of a plant that contains seeds.

Fulcrum (See pivot):

Galaxy: A group of stars.

Gas: A substance with no definite shape or volume. Neither solid nor liquid.

Gastric Juice: Digestive fluid made in the lining of the stomach.

Gears: (gear wheel) a wheel with teeth which increase or decrease the speed of other wheels e.g. gears on a bicycle.

Germs: One-celled, microscopic organisms.

Gill: Breathing organ of a fish.

Gland: An organ, in the body, which produces a fluid.

Gravity: An invisible force attracting objects towards the centre of the earth.

Heart: Muscular organ which pumps blood around the body.

Heart Rate: (Pulse) - the throbbing of blood as it is pumped into the arteries.

Helium: A light gas which does not burn.

Herbivore: Plant eating animal.

Hydrogen: A gas which joins with oxygen to make water.

Ignite: To set on fire, start to burn.

Incisors: Front teeth between the canines.

Incubation: Sitting on eggs in order to hatch them.

Inflammable: Something that is easily set on fire.

Insulator: A material that does not conduct electricity or heat.

Intestines: (small and large) parts of the digestive system.

Invertebrate: Animals without a backbone.

Joints: Where bones join in the skeleton.

Kidneys: The organs, in animals, that filter the blood and produce urine.

Kinetic (energy): energy in the form of movement e.g. a flowing river.

Lever: A bar or pole moving about a fulcrum and used to do work more easily.

Liquid: A substance in a fluid or watery condition. Neither gas nor solid.

Liver: Organ which helps in the digestion of food and the cleansing of blood.

Load (see effort): Part of a lever system. The load is what the lever is trying to move.

Lungs: Breathing organs.

Maggots: Grub or larva of certain insects.

Magnet: A material with a magnetic force which attracts certain metals e.g. iron, cobalt, nickel.

Mammal: Warm-blooded animal, wholly or partly covered with hair or fur. The young are born alive and feed on mother's milk.

Mercury: A silvery metal which is a liquid at room temperature.

Meteors: Bright streaks seen in the sky and often called shooting stars.

Microbes: Very small living organisms.

Molars: Teeth at the back of the jaws.

Mouldy: Covered with a fungus growth.

Mucus: Sticky substance protecting nose etc.

Oesophagus: A tube through which food travels to the stomach.

Opaque: Opaque objects do not let light pass through them.

Glossary continued on inside back cover.

LIFE PROCESSES AND LIVING THINGS 1

(HUMANS)

SCORE: TEST ONE _____

TEST TWO _____

TEST ONE

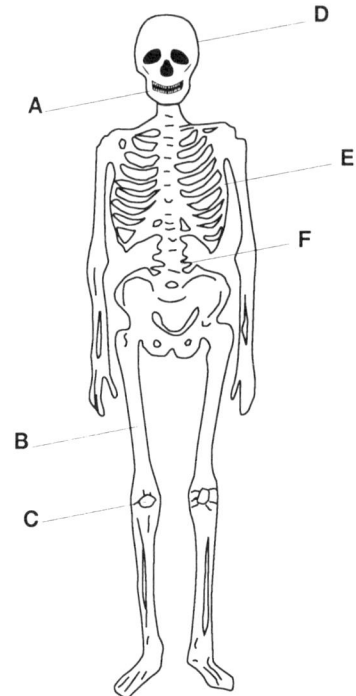

MUSCLES / SKELETON

Name the bones marked A, B and C.

1 A. (_____)

2 B. (_____)

3 C. (_____)

Name the bones marked D, E and F and say which parts of the body they protect.

4 + **5** D (_____) protects the (_____)

6 + **7** E (_____) protects the (_____)

8 + **9** F (_____) protects the (_____)

Bones join together at joints. We have hinge joints, ball and socket joints and gliding joints.
Decide what kind of joint each of the following is.

Example.   Elbow_____Hinge Joint_____

10 Shoulder (_____)   **11** Knee (_____)

12 Spine   (_____)   **13** Hip (_____)

LIFE PROCESSES AND LIVING THINGS 1 PAGE 1

PULL   RELAXES   PUSH   CONTRACTS

Choose words from the above list to complete this short passage.

Our bodies can move because muscles **14** (_____) on bones. To do this one muscle **15** (_____) while at the same time another muscle **16** (_____).

17 Muscles never (_____) on bones.

Anne, Bob and Charles wanted to carry out a test to see who was the most flexible.
This diagram shows what they did and the results they obtained.

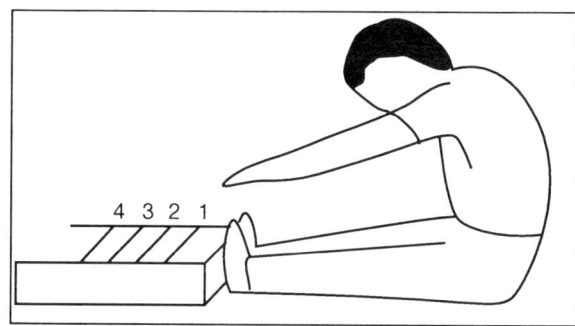

Name	Point reached on scale
Anne	1
Bob	4
Charles	2

Answer these questions:-

18 Which child is most flexible? (_____)

19 Why is this a fair test? Circle your answer.

    (a)   They are all children.   (b)   They can all bend.

    (c)   They all do exactly the same thing.   (d)   They are all 12 years old.

20 David joins in and while standing, legs straight, can place his hands flat on the ground. Circle one statement which is most accurate and connected with the above experiment.

(a) David is 12 years old.   (b) David's flexibility cannot be compared with the others.
(c) David is less flexible than Bob.   (d) David is more flexible than Anne.

LIFE PROCESSES AND LIVING THINGS 1 PAGE 2

HEART

Questions 21-25 are about a normally fit 11 year old boy with a resting heart rate of 75 beats per minute. The following activities affect the rate at which his heart beats. Number them from 1 to 5. Activity number 1 will give him the slowest heart rate and activity 5 will give him the fastest.

	Activity	Number
21	sleeping	(_____)
22	jogging	(_____)
23	running to the top of a sand dune	(_____)
24	standing still	(_____)
25	walking	(_____)

26 Which activity above is represented by the graph below?   (_____)

[Graph showing HEART BEATS per MINUTE vs TIME IN MINUTES. The curve starts at 75, rises to about 140 at around 0.75 minutes, then falls back to 75 by 2 minutes.]

27 Which activity in questions 21-25 may have a rate of less than 75 beats per minute? (_____)

28 Three normally fit 10 year old girls decided to study the effects of exercise on heart rate. One child skipped, another kicked a ball against a wall and the third ran on the spot. Each activity lasted for exactly two minutes. Pulse rates were taken immediately before and after the activities. The increase in each child's pulse rate was calculated and compared with that of the others.

Why was this not a fair test? Tick your answer from the list below.

(a) Two minutes exercise is not enough for an experiment.   ☐
(b) Skipping is more difficult than kicking a ball.   ☐
(c) They all did different activities.   ☐
(d) Girls don't usually play football.   ☐

The heart is a muscular organ which pumps blood around the body. It is divided into two halves - the left and the right side. Each side has two chambers. Look at the simplified diagram below. Write the name of each chamber beside its definition. Arrows show the direction the blood is flowing.

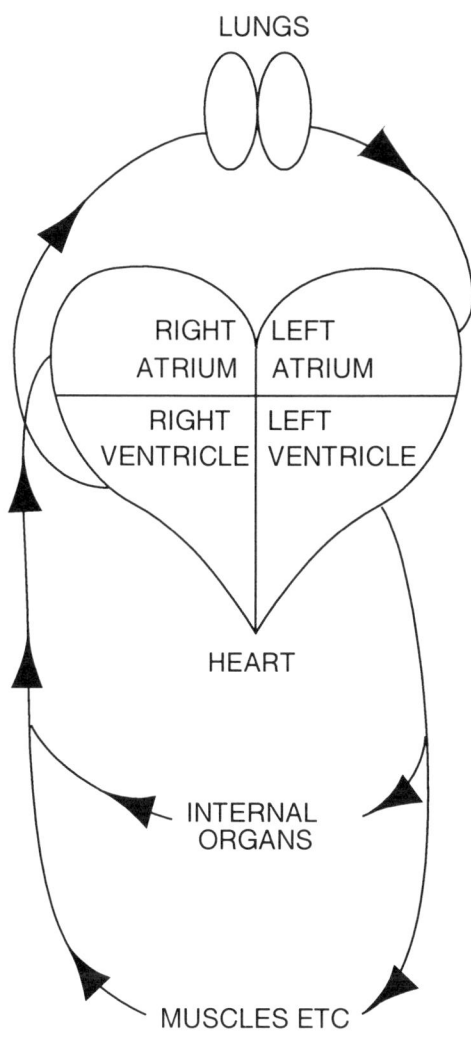

29 Blood returning from the muscles and organs enters here. (_____)

30 From here blood is pumped to the lungs. (_____)

31 Blood is pumped from here to the muscles and organs of the body. (_____)

32 This chamber receives blood coming from the lungs. (_____)

33 Study the list below and tick those things which help to prevent heart disease.

(a) smoking ☐   (b) healthy diet ☐   (c) fatty foods ☐

(d) regular exercise ☐   (e) blocked arteries ☐

KIDNEYS   VEINS   LUNGS   VALVES   ARTERIES   CAPILLARIES

Match the words above to the definitions below.

34 Blood vessels which carry blood away from the heart. (_____)

35 Blood vessels which carry blood back to the heart. (_____)

36 Tiny blood vessels which connect the two larger types of vessels. (_____)

37 Devices which prevent blood from flowing the wrong way in blood vessels. (_____)

38 Where the blood deposits carbon dioxide and picks up oxygen. (_____)

39 Where waste products in the blood stream are removed. (_____)

This graph shows the heart rates of two healthy 25 year old men of similar height and build both doing the same amount of work.

40 Which of these two men is the fitter? (_____)

HEALTHY LIFESTYLE

41 Tick those foods often regarded as containing a lot of calcium.
(a) **Cheese** ☐   (b) **Apples** ☐   (c) **Water** ☐   (d) **Potatoes** ☐   (e) **Milk** ☐   (f) **Carrots** ☐

42 Food can be put into different groups. Put each food below into the correct box.

BUTTER   WHITE BREAD   CHICKEN BREAST

CARBOHYDRATE	PROTEIN	FAT

LIFE PROCESSES AND LIVING THINGS 1 PAGE 5

43 Tick two foods often regarded as containing a lot of sugar.

(a) **tomato ketchup** ☐   (b) **potato crisps** ☐   (c) **chocolate** ☐
(d) **apples** ☐   (e) **potatoes** ☐   (f) **cheese** ☐

44 Tick two foods often regarded as containing a lot of fat.

(a) **bread** ☐   (b) **peach** ☐   (c) **deep fried chips** ☐
(d) **white meat** ☐   (e) **vegetables** ☐   (f) **butter** ☐

Label the teeth in this diagram. Choose from -

INCISORS   CANINES   MOLARS

45 _____

46 _____

47 _____

Suggest 3 ways to keep your teeth healthy.

48 _____

49 _____

50 _____

LIFE PROCESSES AND LIVING THINGS 1 PAGE 6

TEST TWO

BREATHING

Complete this passage using the correct words from the following list.

OXYGEN   DIAPHRAGM   CARBON DIOXIDE   MOUTH   EXPELLED

Air is drawn into the body through the nose and **1** (_____). The air travels to the lungs where **2** (_____) is removed from it. The body produces **3** (_____) and this is **4** (_____) when we breath out. A muscle, below the lungs, called the **5** (_____) helps us to breathe.

Write **True** or **False** to these statements. Write **True** or **False** in the brackets.

6 Air from our lungs helps us to talk.   (_____)

7 Asbestos dust can damage our lungs.   (_____)

8 Cigarette smoke is good for our lungs.   (_____)

9 Breathing in is called inhaling.   (_____)

10 What is the name of the method of providing a room with fresh air? Circle one answer.
INCUBATION   INHALATION   VENTILATION   EXHALATION

11 In a stuffy room which gas tends to make people feel sleepy? (_____)

12 Which gas is essential for human life?   (_____)

Complete this passage using the correct words. Choose from this list.

MORE   LESS   OXYGEN   HYDROGEN

At the top of a high mountain humans find it difficult to breath because there is **13** (_____) **14** (_____) in the air than at sea level.

15 Other things, apart from people, breathe. Study the list below and tick everything that breathes.
(a) salt ☐   (b) tree ☐   (c) water ☐   (d) eagle ☐   (e) fish ☐

It is normally better to breathe through your nose than through your mouth. Give two reasons why this is so.

16 _____

17 _____

LIFE PROCESSES AND LIVING THINGS 1 PAGE 7

Peter and Mark, both aged 16, wanted to see who had the biggest lung capacity. They blew into the tube in one continuous blow.

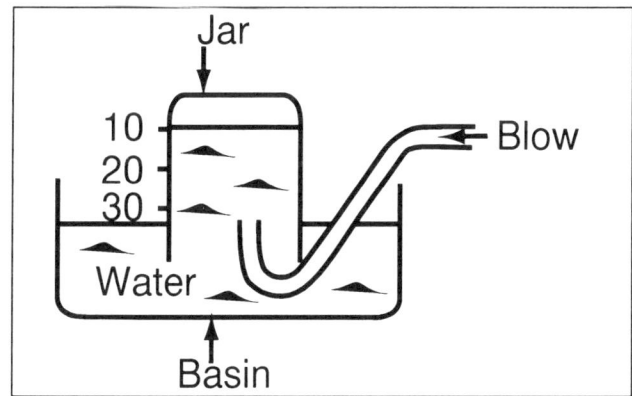

NAME	POINT ON SCALE
PETER	23
MARK	18

18 By reading the results decide who has the biggest lung capacity. (_____)

19 Choose one answer to explain what happened to the water in the **JAR**.

(a) The inhaled air displaced the water. ☐   (b) The exhaled air displaced the water. ☐

(c) The water level rose. ☐   (d) The water level remained unchanged. ☐

20 Choose one answer to explain what happened to the water in the **BASIN**.

(a) The water level went down. ☐   (b) The water level remained unchanged. ☐

(c) The water level rose. ☐   (d) The water cooled down. ☐

DIGESTION

Label this diagram. Choose from this list and place the correct name on each line.

KIDNEY   **STOMACH**   **MOUTH**   **LIVER**
OESOPHAGUS   **SMALL INTESTINE**   **LARGE INTESTINE**

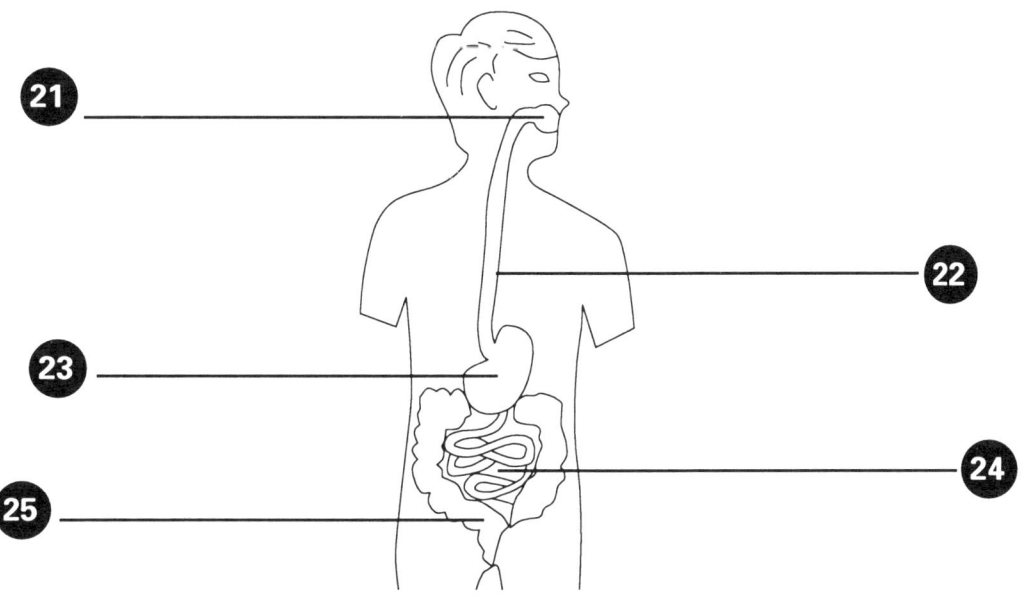

LIFE PROCESSES AND LIVING THINGS 1 PAGE 8

The digestion of food begins in the mouth. Adults have 3 types of teeth each with different uses. Complete the table.

	USE	TOOTH NAME
26	Biting food	
27	Tearing food	
28	Grinding food	

Food is needed to nourish the cells of the body. In order for this to happen it must be broken down and absorbed into the blood. This happens through the process of digestion. The four main stages of digestion are described below but not in the correct order.

Match the descriptions with where they take place and label them using the following words.

SMALL INTESTINE   LARGE INTESTINE   MOUTH   STOMACH

29. Juices from the liver and pancreas enter here. A rippling movement pushes the food along. (_____)

30. Glands make saliva which mixes with the food. (_____)

31. Food that has not been absorbed into the blood stays here and is then passed into the rectum from where it passes out of the body. (_____)

32. Gastric juices are produced here. They mix with the food and churn it into a thick liquid. (_____)

Write **True** or **False** to these statements.

33. The digestive system breaks food down into chemical substances. (_____)

34. Sight or smell of food produces saliva in a hungry person's mouth. (_____)

35. Food is absorbed into the blood stream before travelling to the cells. (_____)

36. It is not possible to digest food standing on your head. (_____)

37. Food is mixed with acids and broken down mainly in the stomach. (_____)

38. Oxygen and food combine to release energy into the cells. (_____)

39. One cause of indigestion may be when food is eaten too (_____) and is swallowed in (_____) chunks.

40. Fibre helps food move through the digestive system. Tick **three** foods which contain a lot of fibre.

    (a) vegetables ☐   (b) meat ☐   (c) fruit ☐
    (d) cheese ☐   (e) wholemeal bread ☐   (f) chocolate ☐

HEALTHY LIFESTYLE

Look at the diagram of a smoking machine. It represents what happens when a person smokes a cigarette. Each part represents some part of the human body. Complete the table below.

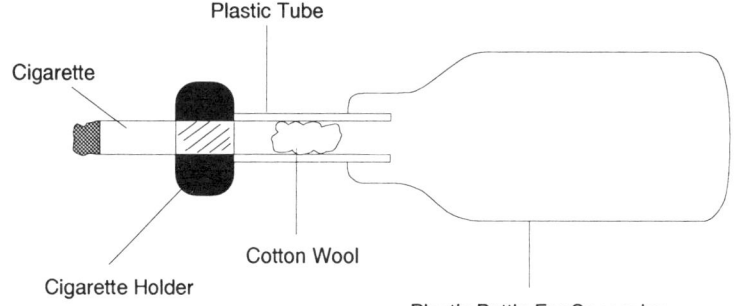

Machine Part		Human Body
41 Cigarette Holder	represents	
42	represents	Airways
43 Plastic bottle	represents	

44 How will the cotton wool change when the cigarette is lit and the bottle squeezed and then released?

_____

45 Name one other way in which people smoke tobacco.

_____

The five sentences below are about how the body can prevent the spread of germs. Complete the sentences correctly. Place the letter of the ending beside the correct beginning. Use each ending only once.

Choose from these endings -

46 Hair and mucus in the nose   (_____)   A   can kill germs in the eye.

47 Saliva in the mouth   (_____)   B   prevents germs entering the blood.

48 Skin covering the body   (_____)   C   can kill germs in the stomach.

49 Blinking   (_____)   D   can kill germs before they enter the stomach.

50 Juices in the digestive system   (_____)   E   stops germs reaching the lungs.

LIFE PROCESSES AND LIVING THINGS 2

(ANIMALS AND PLANTS)

SCORE:　　TEST ONE _____

TEST TWO _____

TEST THREE _____

TEST ONE

1 The animal kingdom is divided into vertebrates and invertebrates. What does one have that the other does not have?

_____

Sort these animals into **vertebrates** and **invertebrates** by writing **V** or **I** beside each name.

2 slug (____) **3** frog (____) **4** wren (____)

5 ape (____) **6** oyster (____) **7** bee (____)

8 – **13** Invertebrates are animals which do not have a backbone. Some do have a skeleton in the form of an outer shell. Place the following invertebrates in the correct boxes below.

SNAIL   SPIDER   BUTTERFLY   CRAB   JELLYFISH   OYSTER

CREATURES WITH A SHELL	CREATURES WITHOUT A SHELL

The stages in the life cycle of a fly are drawn below but not in the correct order. Label the drawings correctly. Choose from these words.

EGGS   PUPAE   ADULT FLY   MAGGOTS

14 (_____)   **15** (_____)

16 (_____)   **17** (_____)

LIFE PROCESSES AND LIVING THINGS 2 PAGE 1

Complete the life cycle of the fly using these words.

EGGS   PUPAE   MAGGOTS

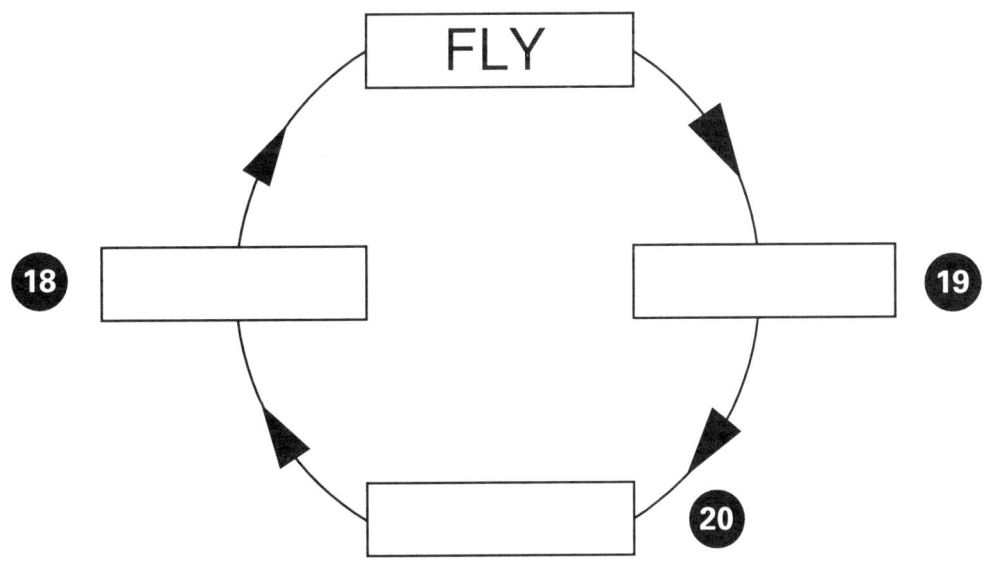

To which part of a fly's body are the following attached?

21 Feelers (_____)

22 Legs (_____)

23 Wings (_____)

Name the three main parts of this insect. Choose from the words below.

HEAD   LEGS   THORAX   STOMACH   ABDOMEN

24 (_____)

25 (_____)

26 (_____)

LIFE PROCESSES AND LIVING THINGS 2 PAGE 2

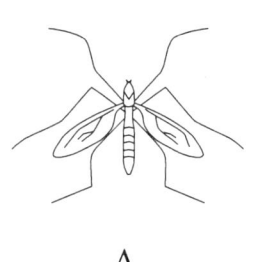 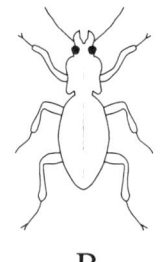 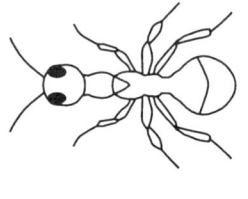 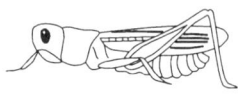

A   B   C   D

Look at these drawings of invertebrates. Use this table and the drawings to decide what each is called.

	Wings	6 Legs	Strong rear legs	All legs on thorax
Crane Fly	✓	✓	✗	✗
Ant	✗	✓	✗	✓
Grasshopper	✓	✓	✓	✗
Beetle	✗	✓	✗	✗

27 A (_____)

28 B (_____)

29 C (_____)

30 D (_____)

Label the parts of an earthworm. Use these words.

SEGMENT   **SADDLE**   **MOUTH**

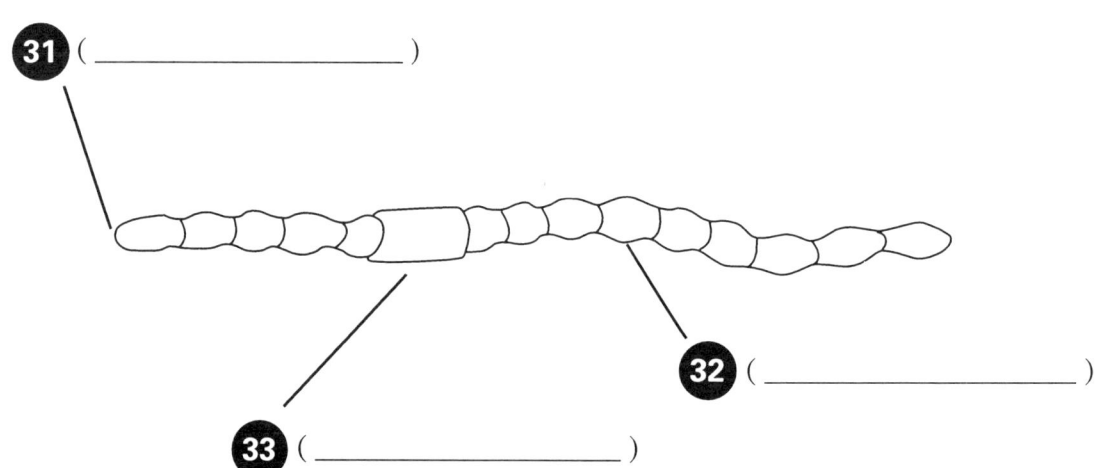

31 (_____)

32 (_____)

33 (_____)

34 Where do worms live? Underline one answer.

a) **Lodges**   b) **Nests**   c) **Burrows**   d) **Dens**

35 What do worms swallow? Underline one answer.

a) **Soil**   b) **Grass**   c) **Leaves**   d) **Insects**.

Questions 36-39 are about earthworms. Decide if each statement is true or false. Write **TRUE** or **FALSE** each time.

36 Earthworms move by shortening and lengthening their body segments. (_____)

37 Earthworms generally stay underground at night. (_____)

38 When an earthworm is cut in half it grows into two new worms. (_____)

39 Earthworms help gardeners by breaking up the soil. (_____)

40 - **45** Use some of the following words to complete the passage about snails.

| PROTECTION | EXTERNAL | EYES | INTERNAL |
| SLIME | TENTACLES | MOLLUSCS | VERTEBRATES |

Snails are invertebrates with an (_____) shell and belong to a group of animals known as (_____). A snail's body is soft and can be withdrawn into the shell for (_____). The snail leaves a trail of (_____) when it moves. It has two sets of (_____) on its head. One set contains (_____).

46 How many parts has a spider's body? Circle your answer.   (1   2   3   4)

47 How many legs has a spider?   (_____)

48 What do spiders spin?   (_____)

49 Which of the following describes all spiders? Tick one box.

   Herbivores ☐   **Predators** ☐   **Vegetarians** ☐   **Plant eaters** ☐

50 What do spiders eat? Tick one box.

   Grass ☐   **Flowers** ☐   **Leaves** ☐   **Insects** ☐

LIFE PROCESSES AND LIVING THINGS 2 PAGE 4

TEST TWO

VERTEBRATES

Vertebrates have backbones and are divided into five groups.

1 - **8** Below is a list of vertebrates. Decide which group each belongs to and complete the table.

SPARROW   **NEWT**   **TROUT**   **TOAD**
COD   **APE**   **SNAKE**   **WREN**

MAMMAL	REPTILE	BIRD	FISH	AMPHIBIAN

FISH

	Lays Eggs	Has Gills	Can live on land for long periods	Has Scales and fins	Has Lungs
FISH	✔	✔	✘	✔	✘

Look at the table above and list the factors that make a fish.

9 _____

10 _____

11 _____

Label the diagram of a fish using these words.

GILLS   SCALES   DORSAL FIN   TAIL FIN

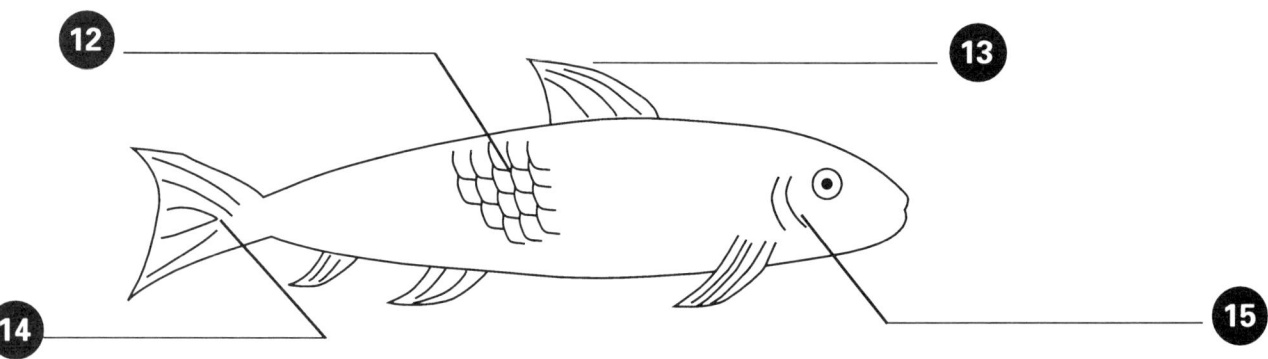

LIFE PROCESSES AND LIVING THINGS 2 PAGE 5

AMPHIBIANS

16 - 18   Tick **three** features below which are true for amphibians.

A) The sun hatches the eggs. ☐

B) They lay soft eggs in water. ☐

C) They breathe with gills when young. ☐

D) Adults can live on land. ☐

E) Amphibians are warm blooded. ☐

Below is the life cycle of a frog but the sentences are not in the correct order. Place the numbers **2-6** in the correct position. Number **1** has been completed for you.

The female lays a mass of eggs.   (1)

19   Front legs appear.   (____)

20   Tadpole emerges from egg.   (____)

21   A tadpole with a short round body and a flat tail appears inside an egg.   (____)

22   Two rear legs are formed.   (____)

23   Leaves water as a young frog.   (____)

REPTILES

24 - 26   Tick **three** features below which make an animal a reptile.

(a) scaley skin ☐

(b) warm blooded ☐

(c) eggs laid in water ☐

(d) cold blooded ☐

(e) eggs laid on land ☐

(f) slimy skin ☐

COLD BLOODED   TEMPERATURE   SUNSHINE   HOT   COLD

Choose words from the above list to complete this passage. Each word may be used only once.

Reptiles are **27** (_____) so their bodies remain at the **28** (_____) of the air or water around them. If they get too **29** (_____) they may die so they crawl into the shade.

If they get too **30** (_____) they go into the **31** (_____) again.

BIRDS

A bird is a vertebrate. Decide which of the following sentences about birds are **true** or **false**. Write **T** or **F** in the brackets.

32 All birds can fly.   (_____)

33 They all have feathers.   (_____)

34 All birds nest in trees.   (_____)

35 Birds hatch from an egg with a hard shell. (_____)

36 Birds are warm blooded.   (_____)

Complete the table below about 6 birds. The Mallard duck has been completed for you.

	CAN FLY	BIRD OF PREY	WEBBED FEET
Mallard Duck	✔	✘	✔
37 Eagle			
38 Sparrow			
39 Penguin			
40 Swan			
41 Robin			

LIFE PROCESSES AND LIVING THINGS 2 PAGE 7

MAMMALS

List 3 things which make an animal a mammal.

42 _____

43 _____

44 _____

Answer **TRUE** or **FALSE** to these statements.

45 All mammals lay eggs. (_____)

46 No mammals can fly. (_____)

47 Some mammals live in the ocean. (_____)

48 A mouse is not a mammal. (_____)

49 People are mammals. (_____)

50 The heaviest mammal is an elephant. (_____)

TEST THREE

PLANTS

Plants and animals are similar in certain ways. Complete the table below. Write **YES** or **NO** in the boxes.

		Animals	Plants
1	Can take gases from the air	Yes	
2	Some can live under water	Yes	
3	Can move about to find food	Yes	
4	Have a brain	Yes	
5	Affected by temperature changes	Yes	
6	Can produce their food within themselves	No	

7 + **8** Many products are made from plants. Sort the following into two groups and write them in the correct boxes.

LEATHER   **COAL**   **SILK**   **PAPER**

Made from plants	Not made from plants

LIFE PROCESSES AND LIVING THINGS 2 PAGE 8

Various parts of plants are used by humans. Which parts do humans most commonly use from the plants in questions 9-14. Choose from these parts.

ROOTS   BARK   STEMS   LEAVES   FLOWERS   FRUIT

9 cork tree   (_____)   **10** cauliflower   (_____)

11 carrot   (_____)   **12** apple tree   (_____)

13 celery   (_____)   **14** cabbage   (_____)

15 + **16** Plants need certain things in order to grow. Study the list below and tick **two** items which are <u>essential</u> for the growth of a plant.

(a) soil ☐   (b) wind protection ☐   (c) light ☐   (d) compost ☐
(e) fertiliser ☐ (f) water ☐   (g) a container ☐ (h) shade ☐

17 In how many of the places below may plants sometimes be seen growing? (_____)

IN A DESERT   **ON ROOF TOPS**   **ON MOUNTAINS**
IN CRACKS IN CEMENT   **UNDER WATER**   **ON ROCKS**

Six statements about plant parts are given below. Which word best describes each statement? Choose your answers from the following.

OXYGEN   FRUITS   LEAVES
ROOTS   FLOWER   CARBON DIOXIDE

18 Holds the plant firmly in the ground.   (_____)

19 Contains chlorophyll and uses light to produce food.   (_____)

20 Sometimes attracts insects.   (_____)

21 Contains seeds.   (_____)

22 Gas that plants take from the air in daytime.   (_____)

23 Gas that plants give off in daytime.   (_____)

24 + **25** Plants can be divided into two groups, those that bear flowers and those that do not. Sort the following plants and write them in the correct boxes.

SEAWEED   DAFFODIL   MOSS   STRAWBERRY

Flowering	Non Flowering

26 Why do some plants have flowers? Underline **one** sentence below.

(a) To provide sweet smells.   (b) To brighten up our gardens.
(c) To help bees make honey.   (d) To produce seeds that will make new plants.
(e) To catch rain water.

LIFE PROCESSES AND LIVING THINGS 2 PAGE 9

Use these definitions to help you label the parts of the flower.

- STYLE - a stalk with a stigma at the top. The style leads into an egg chamber. Style is sometimes called pistil.

- STAMEN - a stalk with an anther on top. A stamen produces pollen.

- SEPALS - Leaflike and in the form of a cup to hold the flower.

- STIGMA - Sticky when ripe. Catches pollen.

- OVARY - Contains ovules which join with pollen to become seeds.

- ANTHER - A pollen-sac. When ripe it releases pollen.

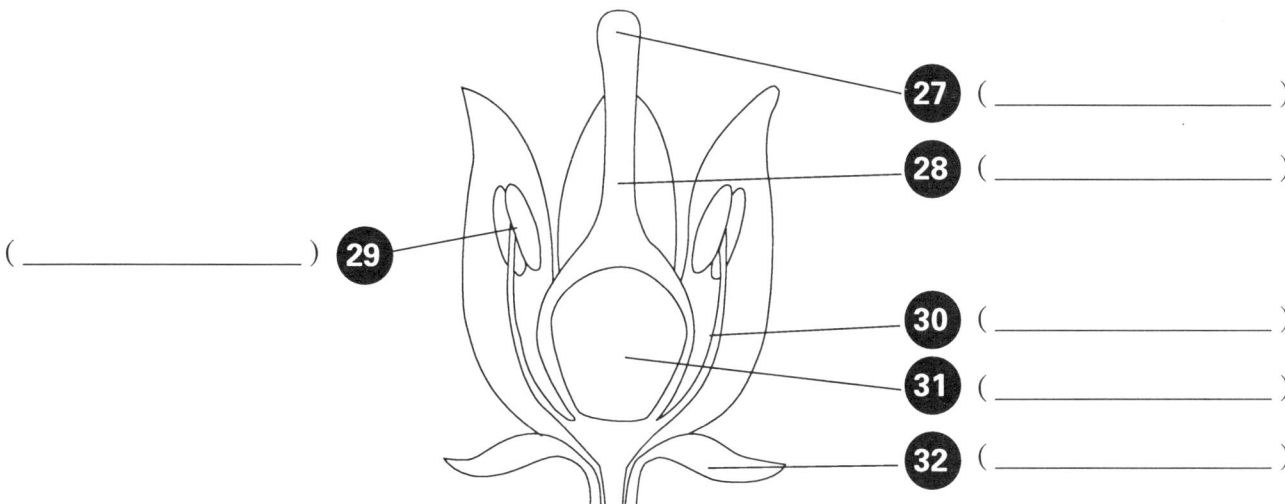

Pollination is when fertilisation takes place and new seeds are formed. In order for this to happen pollen must travel from the stamen to the stigma. Often pollen is carried from one to the other by insects. Give two reasons why insects are attracted to certain plants.

33 _____

34 _____

Give two ways in which pollen is transferred from the stamen to the stigma other than by insects.

35 _____

36 _____

37 A class was studying how insects help to pollinate flowers. They wanted to find out which flower attracted most insects. They grew various types of flower in the school greenhouse under identical conditions and observed how many insects visited each flower. This was a fair test. Which variable was changed in this experiment.?

_____

LIFE PROCESSES AND LIVING THINGS 2 PAGE 10

The seeds of a plant are contained in the fruit of the plant. Decide whether the foods below are fruits or not. Tick **YES** or **NO** each time.

38	Orange	yes ☐	no ☐
40	Gooseberry	yes ☐	no ☐
42	Onion	yes ☐	no ☐

39	Cabbage	yes ☐	no ☐
41	Tomato	yes ☐	no ☐
43	Carrot	yes ☐	no ☐

44 What is the main purpose of fruit? Underline one sentence below.

(a) To be made into jam.   (b) To produce new plants.

(c) To feed birds and animals.   (d) To provide humans with vitamins.

The statements below explain the life cycle of a bean seed. They are not in the correct order. Place them in order by writing the numbers **1-5** beside the correct statements.

45 A seedling appears. (_____)

46 The plant produces flowers. (_____)

47 A bean seed is planted. (_____)

48 The plant grows in size. (_____)

49 Fruit is produced. (_____)

50 Ted wanted to see how well pansy seeds grew in different growing materials. He planted seeds in 4 identical pots. One pot contained soil, one contained sand, one contained peat and the fourth one contained wood chips. All seeds received exactly the same amount of light, heat and water.
Why was this a fair test? Circle one answer.

a) The plants were grown in pots.   b) Pansies are good for experimenting with.

c) Only one variable was changed at a time.   d) The plants were carefully looked after.

MATERIALS AND THEIR PROPERTIES

SCORE: TEST ONE _____

TEST TWO _____

TEST ONE

Complete the table about the properties of LIQUIDS, SOLIDS and GASES.
Answer **YES** or **NO**. One answer has been given for you.

	Has a size	Has a shape	Takes on the shape of its container
1 SOLID	YES		
2 LIQUID			
3 GAS			

4 Underline any liquids in this list of materials.

    sugar   brine   mercury   bronze   tin   milk.

5 Underline any solids in this list of materials.

    water   nitrogen   cork   wood   oil   brass.

6 Underline any gases in this list of materials.

    carbon dioxide   water   tin   helium   oxygen   sand.

7 Underline any materials which dissolve in water.

    sand   pebbles   sugar   glass   stone   salt.

8 + 9 Some materials occur naturally and others are manmade.
Write the following materials in the proper boxes below.

    gold   glass   cotton   steel   plastic   milk.

NATURAL	MANMADE

List the materials below into 2 groups. One for metals and one for non-metals.

    hydrogen   plastic   tin   lead   diamond   gold

10 Metals _____

11 Non-metals _____

12 What are ice and steam different forms of? _____

13 Why are some of the drills used in oil wells tipped with diamond? Circle your answer.

    a)   diamond is very shiny   b)   diamond is very hard
    c)   diamond is very soft   d)   diamond is very expensive

14 A group of children decided to test how quickly different materials dried after being soaked. Samples of wool, linen and silk measuring 10cm x 10cm were soaked in water and then placed in various places in the classroom. Regular checks were made on the materials until they had all dried out. The time taken for each to dry was recorded. Why was this not a fair test?

MATERIALS AND THEIR PROPERTIES   PAGE 1

Match the definitions of various properties with the words from this list. Use each word only once.

FLEXIBLE   SHINY   OPAQUE   ROUGH   TRANSPARENT   RIGID

15. Light does not pass through it.   (_____)
16. Can be easily bent.   (_____)
17. Reflects light.   (_____)
18. Coarse or uneven surface.   (_____)
19. Difficult to bend.   (_____)
20. Light passes through it.   (_____)

A WINDOW PANE   A COMPASS   A CONCRETE POST   A RUBBER BALL   PAPER TOWELS

Match the objects above to the properties below. Use each object only once.

21. Magnetic   (_____)
22. Absorbent   (_____)
23. Flexible   (_____)
24. Transparent   (_____)
25. Strong   (_____)

Sort these materials into two groups. One for **FLEXIBLE** and one for **RIGID**.

RUBBER   COAL   WIRE   IRON

26. Flexible (_____)   27. Rigid (_____)

28. Put these objects in order of weight - heaviest first. Each material is made up as a 1cm cube.

PLASTIC   GLASS   BALSA WOOD   LEAD

_____

29. Which is the heaviest? Underline your answer.

a) a cubic metre of wet soil

b) a cubic metre of foam rubber

c) a cubic metre of dry sand

When some materials are changed the change is permanent. In other materials the change may only be a temporary one. Decide whether the following actions result in a **permanent** or a **temporary** change. Write **P** or **T** on the line.

30. Boiling an egg   (_____)   31. Freezing peas   (_____)
32. Boiling water   (_____)   33. Baking a potato   (_____)
34. Developing a photograph   (_____)   35. Making concrete   (_____)

MATERIALS AND THEIR PROPERTIES PAGE 2

36-40 Complete the passage below by putting each word in the correct space.

Evaporate   Solid   Melts   Gas   Liquid

When a solid is heated it _____ and becomes a _____. When a liquid dries up it is said to _____ and it becomes a _____. Freezing a liquid will change it into a _____.

What is happening in questions 41-43? Choose from this list.

a) A SOLID becomes a LIQUID   b) A GAS becomes a LIQUID

c) A LIQUID becomes a GAS   d) A LIQUID becomes a SOLID

Example: Steam hits a cold mirror (_____A gas becomes a liquid_____)

41 Water is boiled   (_____)

42 Chocolate is melted   (_____)

43 Milk is frozen   (_____)

44 A girl wanted to find out how long it took different liquids to freeze. Containers of milk, water, lemonade and washing up liquid were placed side by side in a freezer. The liquids were examined every five minutes until they had all frozen.

Which two factors below would make this a fair test? Tick your answers.

a) freezer door must not be kept open for too long a time   ☐

b) containers must be identical   ☐

c) containers must be placed on bottom shelf   ☐

d) freezer must not contain anything else   ☐

e) same quantity of each liquid must be used   ☐

45 What do humans take from air in order to live?   (_____)

46 What waste gas do humans breathe out?   (_____)

47 Where in a heated room would you most likely find the warmest air? Underline your answer.

(a) near the windows   (b) near the floor
(c) near the ceiling   (d) near the door.

Cabbage water can be used to test whether a substance is an acid or an alkaline. If the cabbage water turns red it shows the presence of an acid. An alkaline colours the cabbage water blue.

What colour would show if each of the following was added to cabbage water? Write **RED** or **BLUE** on the line.

48 Vinegar   (_____)

49 Lemon Juice   (_____)

50 Bicarbonate of soda (_____)

TEST TWO

Put these materials into the correct boxes. All materials are at room temperature.

1 - 3 Hydrogen   Mercury   Paper   Oxygen   Oil   Sugar

LIQUID	SOLID	GAS

4 + 5 List these materials in the correct boxes.

Nylon   Wool   Leather   Polythene   Silver   Cardboard

MAN MADE	NATURAL

Materials must be suitable for the required task. Tick one answer each time.

6 Wellington boots are made from rubber because

a) rubber is produced in many colours. ☐

b) rubber is easy to produce. ☐

c) rubber is waterproof. ☐

7 Electrical cables have plastic coatings because

a) plastic does not conduct electricity. ☐

b) plastic does conduct electricity. ☐

c) plastic is strong. ☐

8 Ships' chains are made from steel because

a) steel is shiny. ☐

b) steel is plentiful. ☐

c) steel is strong. ☐

MATERIALS AND THEIR PROPERTIES PAGE 4

Materials have different properties. From the list below place each material against its most obvious property. Use each material only once.

GLASS   FIBREGLASS   COPPER   CONCRETE   RUBBER   TISSUE PAPER

9. (_____) can conduct electricity.

10. (_____) is transparent.

11. (_____) is a good heat insulator.

12. (_____) is strong.

13. (_____) is absorbent.

14. (_____) is waterproof.

15 + 16. Which of these objects can be attracted to a magnet? Circle your answers.

(a) plastic pen   (b) steel nail   (c) aluminium saucepan

(d) wooden chair   (e) copper pipe   (f) iron bucket

17. Charlie and Janet conducted an experiment to decide which type of kitchen paper was most absorbent. Charlie spilt milk and dried it up with 3 different kitchen papers. Janet spilt water and dried it up with 3 different kitchen papers. They then calculated how much liquid had been absorbed by each of the six paper types.

Which statement below informs you that this was not a fair test? Tick your answer.

a) Various kitchen papers were used. ☐
b) Different liquids were used. ☐
c) Janet's paper absorbed most liquid. ☐

CONDENSES   MELT   EVAPORATE   BOIL   IGNITE   INFLAMMABLE

Choose the correct word from the above list to complete these sentences.

18. When a liquid dries up it is said to   (_____)

19. When something starts to burn it is said to   (_____)

20. When ice turns to water it is said to   (_____)

21. When steam hits a cold mirror it   (_____)

22. When water is heated to 100°C it will   (_____)

23. Something that is easily set on fire is said to be   (_____)

24 - 29.   **CLOUDS   EVAPORATE   RIVERS   RAIN   SUN   CONDENSES**

Using the words above complete this passage.

The water cycle occurs when the _____ heats the sea and causes the water to _____ . This vapour rises from the sea and _____ into tiny drops of water. The droplets group together and form _____ . When these droplets become heavy enough they fall as _____ which runs into _____ and then into the sea.

Look at this experiment:-

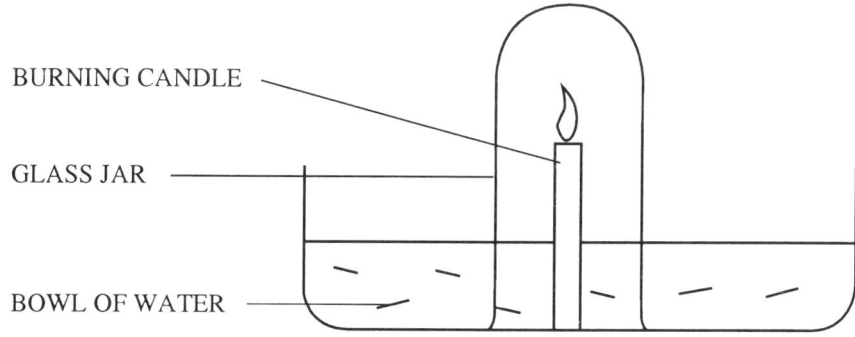

30 After a short time the candle goes out. Why does the candle go out? Tick the correct answer.

(a) The air in the jar becomes damp. ☐
(b) The water puts the candle out. ☐
(c) There is no oxygen left in the jar. ☐

31 What happened to the water level in the glass jar during the experiment? Tick the correct answer.

(a) Level remained unchanged. ☐
(b) Level went down. ☐
(c) Level went up. ☐

32 Which gas has been burnt? (_____)

Answer **TRUE (T)** or **FALSE (F)** to the following statements.

33 Air contains oxygen which we need in order to live. (____)

34 Air pressure is higher on a mountain top than at sea level. (____)

35 A fire needs carbon dioxide in order to burn. (____)

36 Air contains moisture. (____)

37 All living things breathe. (____)

Materials can be changed into new materials. Read the following and decide what each is mainly made from.

Example: Bread is made from (___FLOUR___)

38 Cheese is made from (_____)

39 Glass is made from (_____)

40 Paper is made from (_____)

41 Pottery is made from (_____)

42 Tick those materials which will decompose over time if buried in wet soil.

(a) plastic bag ☐ (b) cabbage leaves ☐
(c) newspaper ☐ (d) car tyre ☐

43 Tick **TWO** factors that may increase the rate of decay of vegetable matter.

(a) cold temperatures ☐
(b) presence of microbes ☐
(c) dry air ☐
(d) warm temperatures ☐

Rusting requires two conditions. What are they?

44 (_____) **45** (_____)

The diagrams below show iron nails in three different containers.

A
Sealed container full of water.

B
Sealed container full of oil.

C
Open container half full of water.

Choose A, B or C to answer these 3 questions.

After 6 months -

46 which nail is badly rusted? (_____)

47 which nail has no rust? (_____)

48 which nail has slight rust? (_____)

Give two methods of preventing rust.

49 _____

50 _____

MATERIALS AND THEIR PROPERTIES PAGE 7

PHYSICAL PROCESSES

SCORE: TEST ONE _____

TEST TWO _____

TEST THREE _____

TEST ONE

Complete the passage below using words from this list.

EARTH	GASES	GALAXY
ENERGY	STAR	SOLID

1 - 6 The sun is a gigantic mass of flaming (_____). It contains no (_____) or liquid material. Although it is about 150 million kilometres from the (_____) it is our nearest (_____). The sun provides (_____) for all living things on earth. The Milky Way (_____) is made up of our sun and millions of other stars.

Our Solar System is made up of the sun, nine planets and their moons, numerous comets, meteors and asteroids. List the names of the planets starting with the one nearest to the sun. Some names have been given to help you.

(**MERCURY**) **7** (_____) **8** (_____)
9 (_____) (**JUPITER**) **10** (_____)
11 (_____) (**NEPTUNE**) **12** (_____)

13 - 16 Complete this passage by circling the correct word in each bracket.

The (**TILT/ ROTATION**) of the earth causes us to have day and night. In the summer month of June in the (**NORTHERN / SOUTHERN**) hemisphere some areas of land may experience little or no (**DAYLIGHT / DARKNESS**). This land is sometimes referred to as the land of the "MIDNIGHT SUN". In (**DECEMBER / MARCH**) the north pole receives no sunshine at all.

Answer **TRUE (T)** or **FALSE (F)** to these statements.

17 Night time occurs because the earth revolves around the sun. (____)

18 There are more hours of daylight in summer than in spring. (____)

19 Towns in northern Scotland get more hours of summer daylight than towns in southern England. (____)

20 If you live in Britain the sun will always be to the north of you. (____)

21 Imaginary lines called lines of latitude help divide the world into different time zones. (____)

22 The shortest day in Britain is in February. (____)

The amount of daylight hours varies throughout the year. For someone living in Britain place these dates in order of hours of daylight. Begin with the day having the most hours of daylight.

29th November   21st September   30th June   15th July   25th December   5th August

23 (_____)   **24** (_____)

25 (_____)   **26** (_____)

27 (_____)   **28** (_____)

29 A class of 11 year olds wanted to see how the length of a shadow, cast by a stick, varied over a month. Tick one factor which would help to make this a fair test.

a) Different sticks to be used. ☐

b) Measurements taken at the same time each day. ☐

c) Shadow must be at least one metre long. ☐

d) Stick to be put in a different position each day. ☐

30 - 37 Complete the passage below using all the words from this list.

LONG   SUN   SHORT   WINTER
TILT   SUMMER   EARTH   WARMER

The seasons are caused by the (_____) of the (_____) as it travels

around the (_____). In (_____) Britain is tilted away from the sun.

Days are (_____) and nights are (_____). When Britain tilts towards the sun

the days are longer and it is (_____). The days are (_____).

PHYSICAL PROCESSES PAGE 2

This diagram shows the revolution of the earth around the sun. If you live in the northern hemisphere which position of earth, on the diagram, will be your **SUMMER / AUTUMN / WINTER / SPRING**? Circle the correct answers.

38 Summer / Autumn / Winter / Spring

39 Summer / Autumn / Winter / Spring

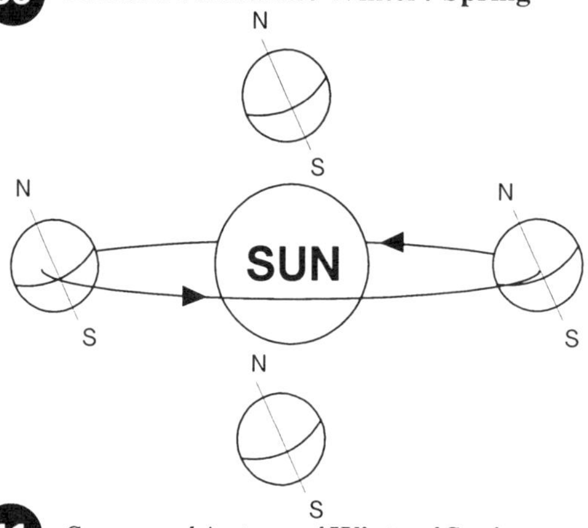

40 Summer / Autumn / Winter / Spring

41 Summer / Autumn / Winter / Spring

Tick one answer to each of the following.

42 In Australia summer includes the month of -

a) July ☐   b) December ☐
c) September ☐   d) March ☐

43 In England spring includes the month of -

a) June ☐   b) April ☐
c) August ☐   d) November ☐

44 In England the day with the least hours of daylight is about -

a) 22nd September ☐   b) 21st June ☐
c) 21st December ☐   d) 21st March ☐

In the northern hemisphere during which seasons are the following likely to occur?
Write **WINTER, SPRING, SUMMER or AUTUMN** each time:

45 Some trees lose their leaves in   _____

46 Some animals hibernate during   _____

47 The day with the greatest amount of daylight is in   _____

48 The day with the least amount of day light is in   _____

49 Outdoor daffodils bloom in   _____

50 The mornings and evenings are dark in   _____

PHYSICAL PROCESSES PAGE 3

TEST TWO

Look at the diagrams of different objects on a balance beam. Tick (✔) each beam which is correct and cross (✘) each beam which is wrong.

1

2

3

4

Look at these diagrams of seesaws with children on them.

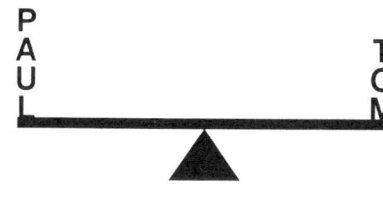

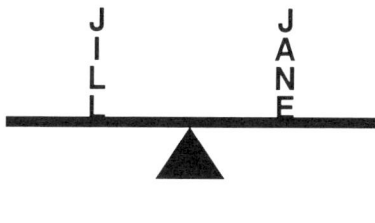

5 Which child is twice as heavy as Tom? (_____)

6 Which child is half as heavy as Paul? (_____)

Decide if each statement is true or false. Write **TRUE** or **FALSE** each time.

7 Paul and Tom are the same weight. (_____)   **8** Anne is lighter than Tom. (_____)

9 Jill is heavier than Jane. (_____)   **10** Paul is heavier than Jill. (_____)

PHYSICAL PROCESSES PAGE 4

A magnet has two ends or poles. The poles are called north and south.
The poles of magnets ATTRACT each other or REPEL each other.
Write **ATTRACT** or **REPEL** below each pair of magnets.

11 | N | S | | N | S |

(_____)

12 | S | N | | N | S |

(_____)

13 | N | S | | S | N |

(_____)

14 | S | N | | S | N |

(_____)

15 What is the name given to the area covered by the lines of force of a magnet?

_____

This diagram shows an electrical device. A pure iron nail has wire wound around it and the wires are connected to 2 batteries.

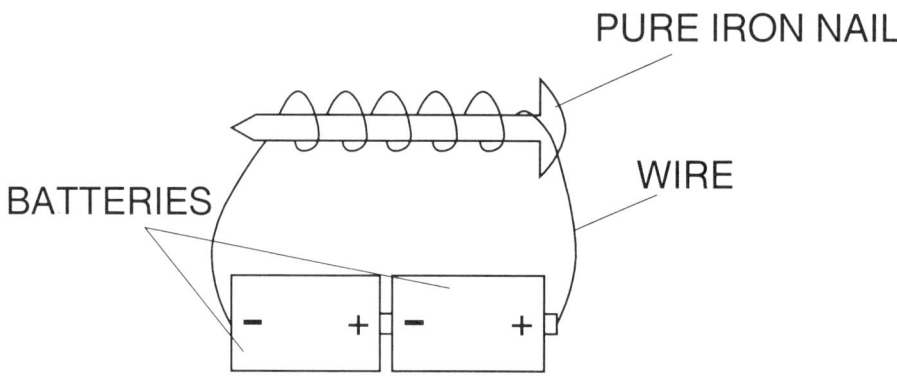

16 What is this device called? Circle one answer.

A) A COMPASS   B) A MAGNET   C) A POLE   D) AN ELECTROMAGNET

17 How could the device above be made stronger? Circle one answer.

A) Use 4 batteries.

B) Decrease the number of turns of wire around the nail.

C) Use a glass rod.

18 Look at the diagram of a crane in a scrap metal yard. One part of it is a large electromagnet. Circle the letter which points to the electromagnet.

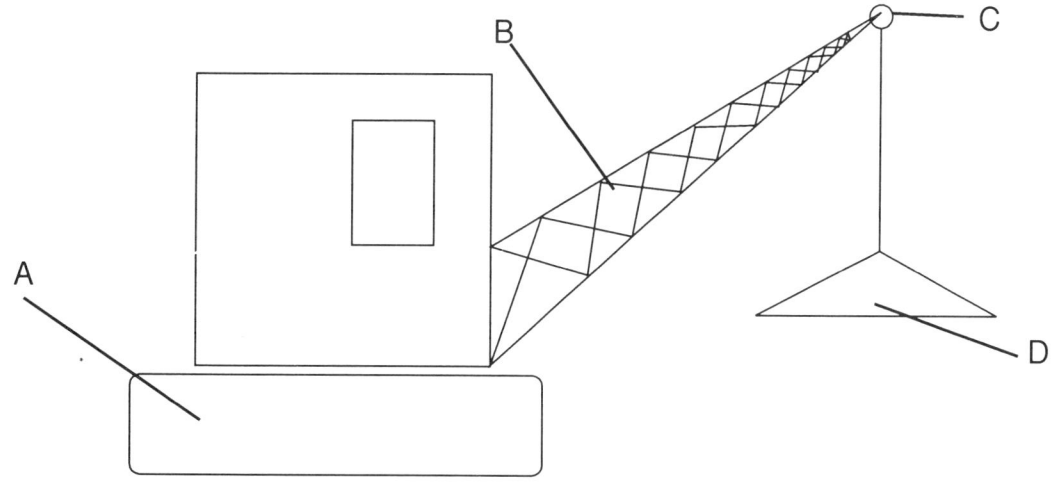

19 + 20 Conductors allow electricity to pass through whilst insulators do not.

Write these materials in the correct boxes.

Plastic fork **Lead pipe** **Cork**
Rubber ball **Steel** **Aluminium foil**

INSULATORS	CONDUCTORS

21 Only one pair of these batteries will work if used in an electrical circuit. Circle the correct answer.

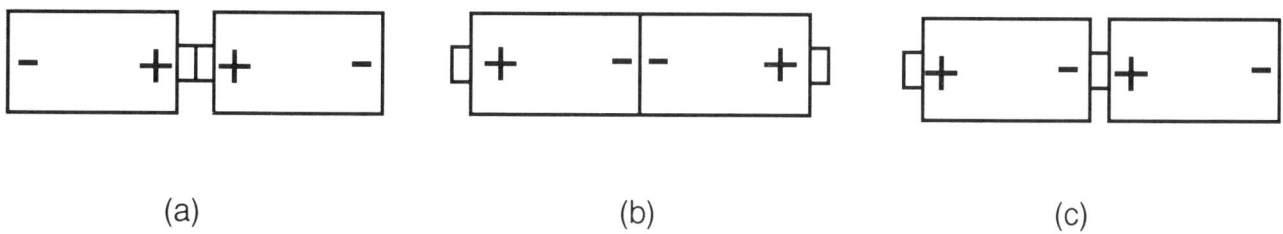

(a)   (b)   (c)

PHYSICAL PROCESSES PAGE 6

Some of these bulbs will light and some will not light. Write **YES** or **NO** in the brackets.

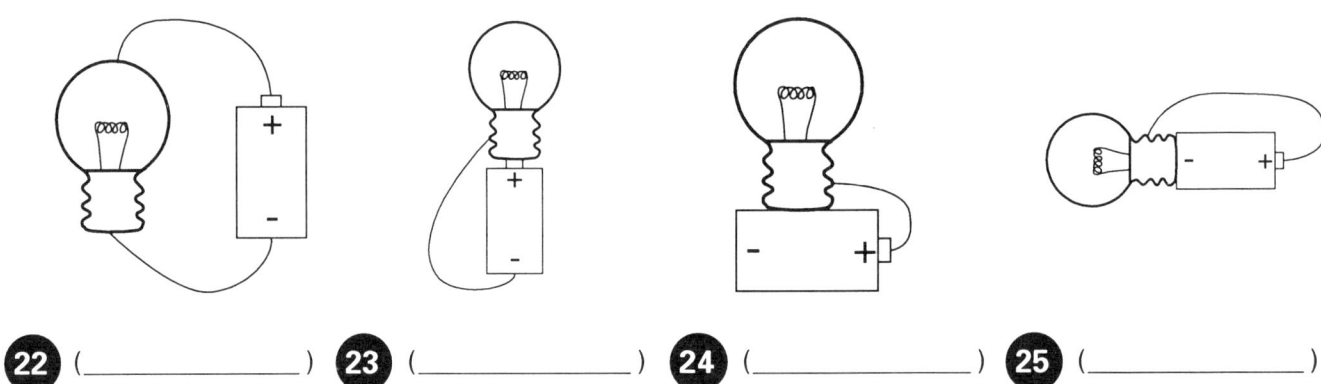

22 (_____) **23** (_____) **24** (_____) **25** (_____)

The following symbols are used to represent various parts of electrical circuits.

A bulb in its holder   A switch (open)   A switch (closed)   A battery

Which of the circuits in questions 26-29 will cause the bulb to light? Tick **YES** or **NO** in each question.

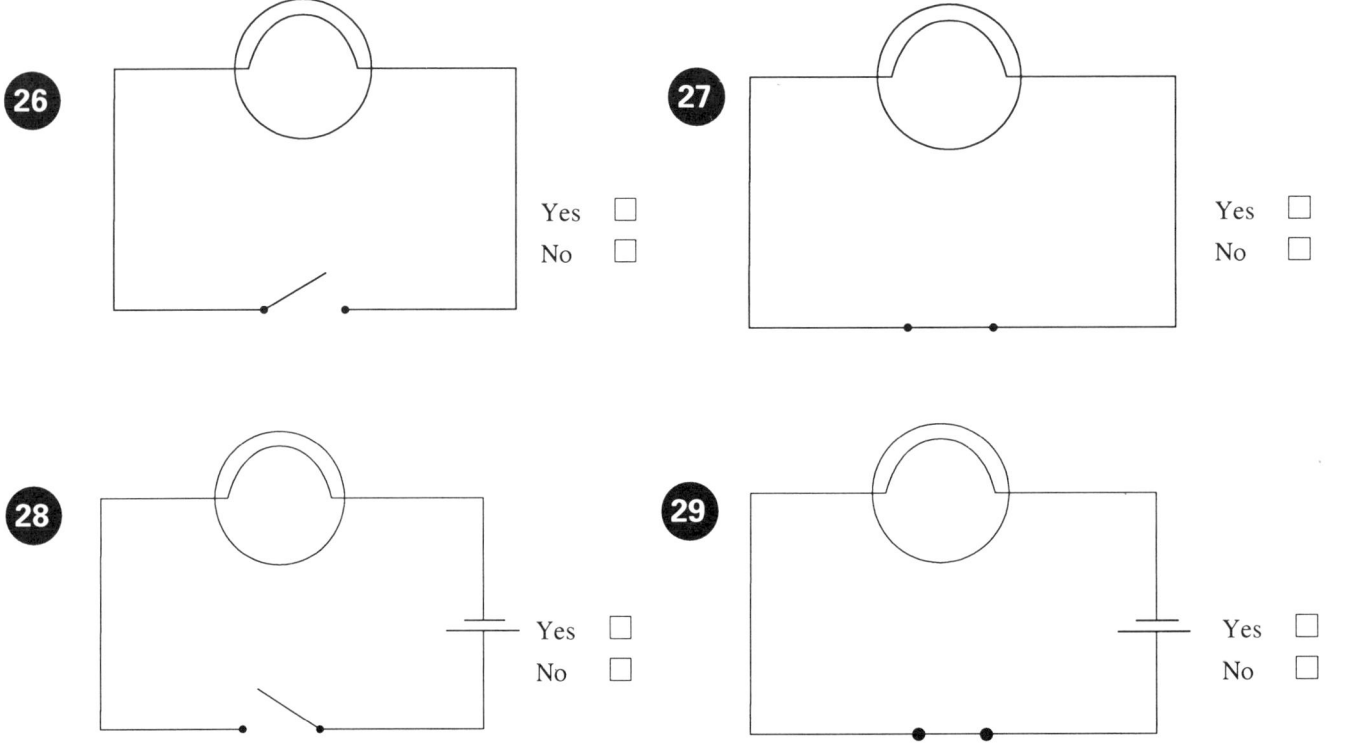

26 Yes ☐ No ☐

27 Yes ☐ No ☐

28 Yes ☐ No ☐

29 Yes ☐ No ☐

Give **2** reasons why some of the bulbs in the circuits will not light.

30 _____

31 _____

PHYSICAL PROCESSES PAGE 7

White light can be split into a series of colours by using a glass prism.
Complete the list by inserting the missing colours.

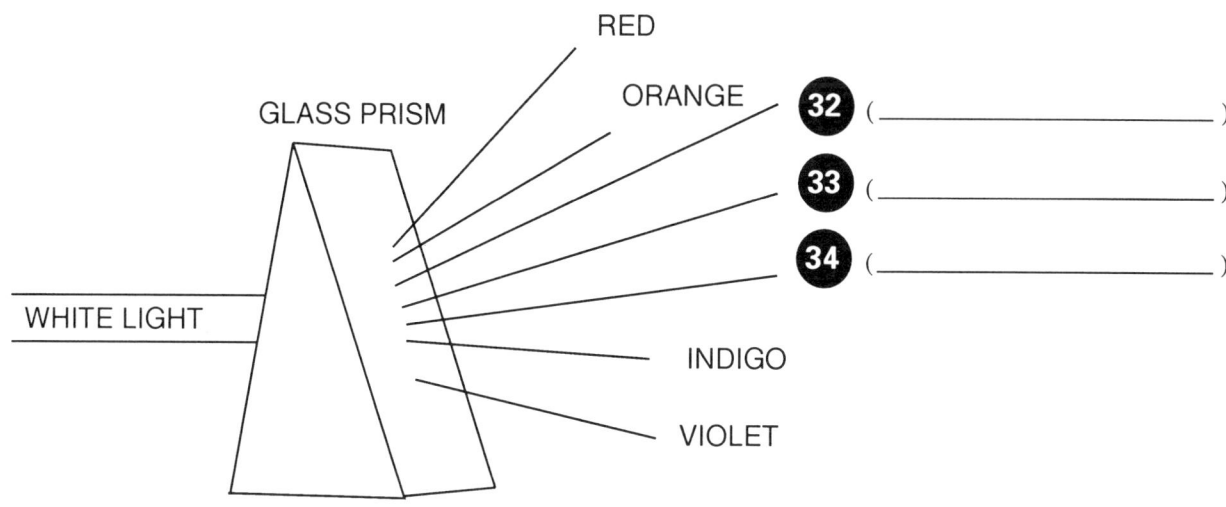

32 (_____)
33 (_____)
34 (_____)

Light travels in a straight line. Look at these periscopes and say in which direction the person can see. Choose from -

FORWARDS   BACKWARDS   NO DIRECTION.

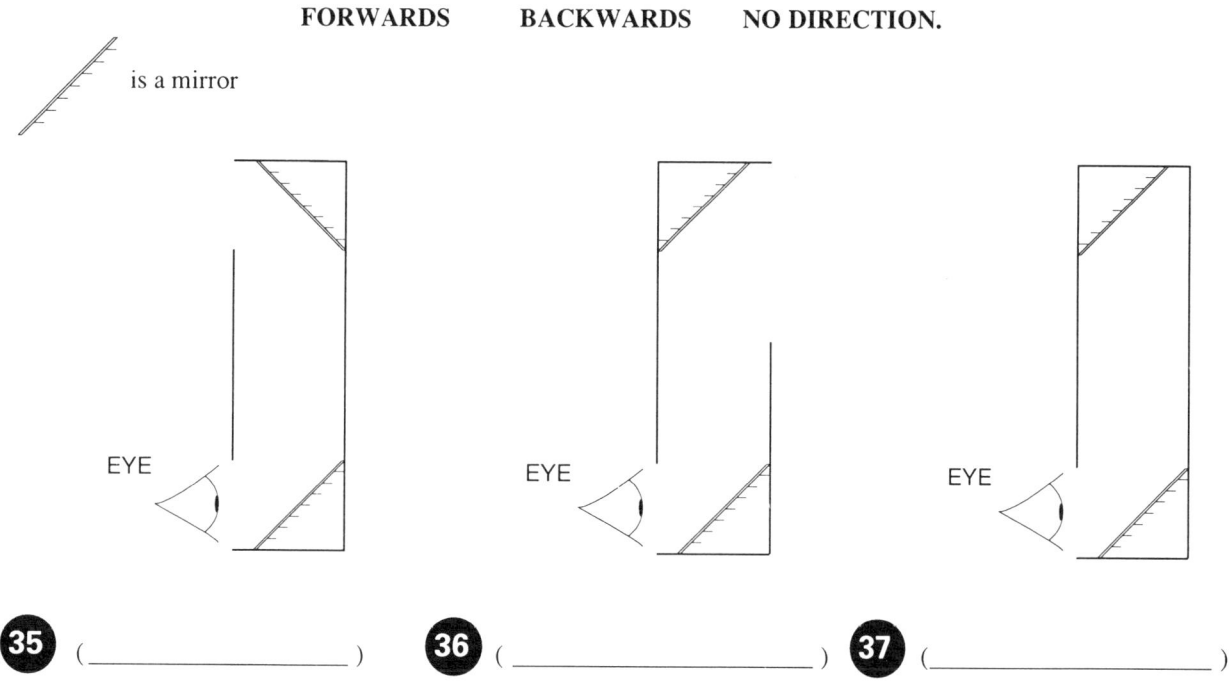

35 (_____)   36 (_____)   37 (_____)

38 Tom, Jean, Janet and Jill investigated which materials allowed most light to pass through. Tom used a candle, Jean used a torch, Janet a slide projector and Jill a table lamp as their sources of light. They all used squares of cardboard, linen and newspaper in their experiments. Why was this not a fair test? Tick your answer.

a) Cardboard is thicker than newspaper. ☐
b) A candle is not very bright. ☐
c) Different sources of light were used. ☐
d) The torch had weak batteries. ☐

39 + 40 Some machines operate mainly by **PUSHING** and others mainly by **PULLING**. Study the machines below and decide whether they work by **PUSHING** or **PULLING**. Place the machines in the correct boxes.

JET ENGINES **CAR TOWING CARAVAN** **BULLDOZER** **TRACTOR WITH PLOUGH**

PUSHING	PULLING

41 + 42 A force is a push or a pull. Study the actions below. Write the letter of each action in the correct box.

A) Wheeling a pram.
B) Picking a flower.
C) Taking a sweet from a bag.
D) Sticking a stamp on a letter.
E) Wind blowing smoke.
F) Tug of war.

PUSHING	PULLING

43 - 47 Using the words below complete the following passage about gravity.

FALL   **CENTRE**   **FORCE**   **SURFACE**   **SPACE**

Gravity is an invisible (_____) which pulls everything towards the (_____) of the earth. If there was no gravity, objects would leave the (_____) of the earth and go into (_____). Gravity causes things to (_____) towards the ground.

48 - 50 The 6 statements below are about gravity. Only **3** are correct. Tick those statements which are **CORRECT**.

A) Gravity is less at night. ☐
B) Gravity on our moon is about 1/6th the strength of gravity on earth. ☐
C) Gravity does not affect an aeroplane at take-off. ☐
D) Gravity only affects living things. ☐
E) Gravity holds you back when you cycle up hill. ☐
F) The gravitational pull of our moon affects tides on earth. ☐

TEST THREE

Sound is caused by something vibrating. Look at the list of musical instruments below and say what is vibrating each time?

1 violin (_____)

2 recorder (_____)

3 drum (_____)

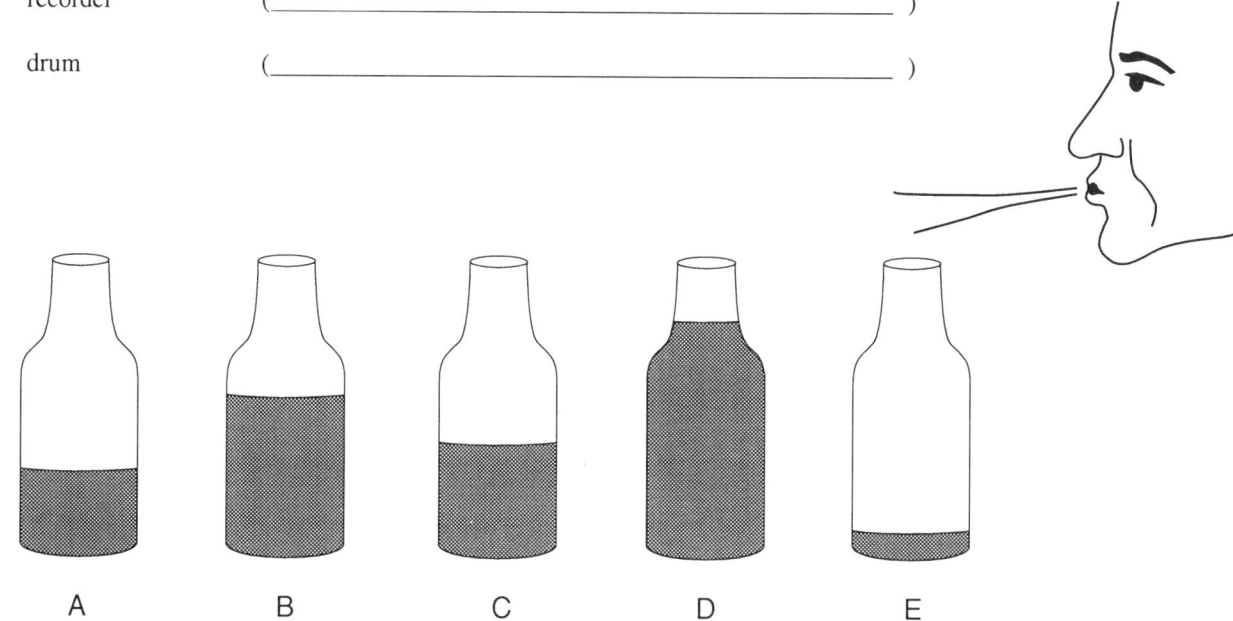

By blowing across the top of a bottle a note is sounded. When water is in the bottle the note is changed. Five bottles with different amounts of water are shown above.

4 Which bottle produces the lowest note? (_____)

5 Which bottle produces the highest note? (_____)

6 What vibrates in the bottles to produce the notes? (_____)

A STRING TELEPHONE

7 + 8 Yogurt cartons and six different types of string were used by a class of children to make string telephones. They wanted to known which type of string made the best telephone.

Which **TWO** factors below ensured that this was a fair test. Underline your answers.

A) The same two children tried all the telephones.

B) The yogurt cartons were big enough to fit over the children's ears.

C) The children recited poems to each other.

D) Ten metres of string was used for each telephone.

E) The children did not shout.

PHYSICAL PROCESSES PAGE 10

Write **True** or **False** in the brackets.

9 An echo is a sound being reflected back. (_____)

10 Sounds cannot travel around obstacles. (_____)

11 We know the direction a sound comes from because we have two ears. (_____)

12 Some creatures use sound to help them move about. (_____)

13 Sound travels faster than light. (_____)

14 Sound can travel through a vacuum. (_____)

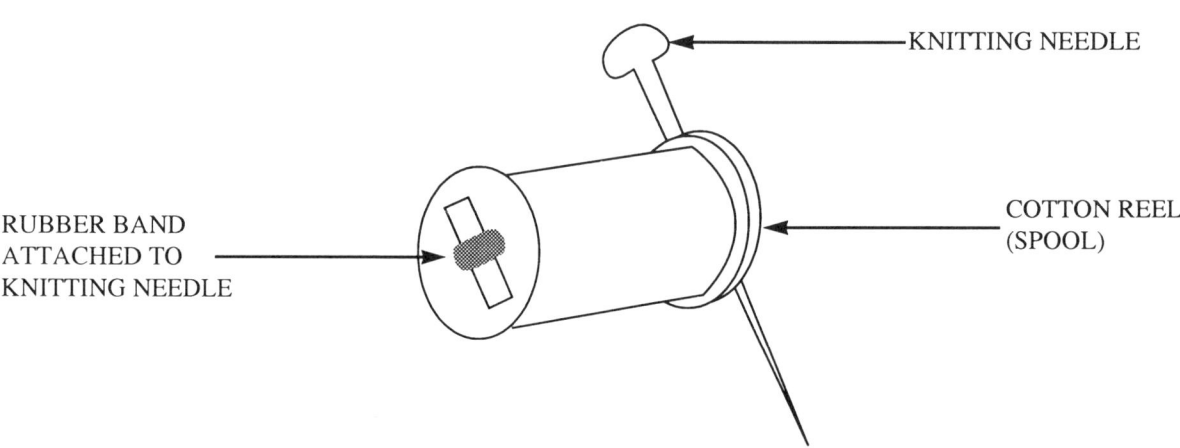

15 This toy was used in an experiment by three children to see how far it would travel on grass, carpet and on a concrete path. The children took it in turns to use the toy on each surface. The elastic band was twisted 12 times before releasing the toy. The distances travelled were measured and recorded. Why was this a fair test? Tick one answer.

a) A toy like this is cheap to make. ☐

b) All the children did the same thing. ☐

c) The children wrote about what happened. ☐

d) Toys are good for experimenting with. ☐

16 - 21 Energy can be divided into 2 groups - **POTENTIAL** and **KINETIC** energy. Stored energy is known as **POTENTIAL** energy and energy in the form of movement is known as **KINETIC** energy.

Study the sources of energy below and decide whether they are **POTENTIAL** energy or **KINETIC** energy. Place them in the correct boxes.

A RIVER   **COAL**   **FOOD**   **WIND**   **BATTERY**   **GAS**

POTENTIAL ENERGY	KINETIC ENERGY

A lever is a simple machine which is used to move a load by applying effort over a pivot. Label the wheelbarrow and nut cracker. An example has been given. The diagrams are not drawn to scale.

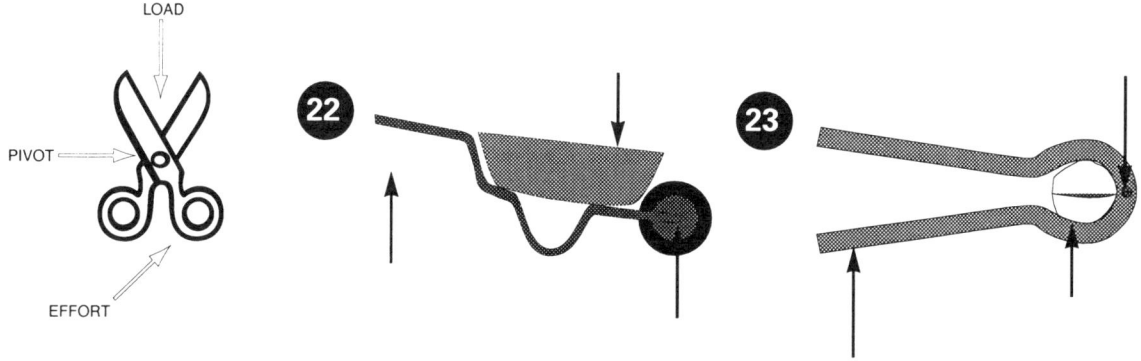

Gears and drive belts are often used in machines. Look at these diagrams and answer the questions. Wheel A has 24 teeth and Wheel B has 12 teeth.

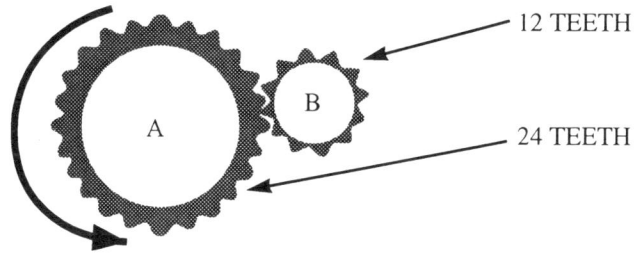

24 If wheel A turns once, how many times would wheel B turn? (_____)

25 In which direction would wheel B turn? Circle your answer.   **CLOCKWISE / ANTICLOCKWISE**

26 + **27** Look at this diagram of 3 wheels and two belts.

The direction B is turning is marked on the diagram. Mark the directions in which A and C are turning on the diagram.

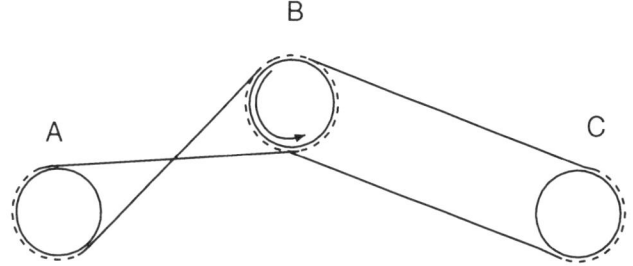

PHYSICAL PROCESSES PAGE 12

Friction is a force which tries to stop objects moving. Some activities or actions require friction while others do not. In the following say where the friction mainly occurs.

Example: When a car is stopping friction occurs between (___**TYRES**___) and (___**ROAD**___).

28 When a parachutist is floating down friction occurs between (_____) and (_____).

29 When an ice-skater is skating friction occurs between (_____) and (_____).

30 When writing on a blackboard friction occurs between (_____) and (_____).

Write **YES** if friction is desirable and **NO** if friction is not desirable.

31 When a car engine is working.   (_____)   **32** A sprinter running on a track.   (_____)

33 When applying brakes on a bicycle. (_____)   **34** A car trying to go up a snow covered hill. (_____)

35 In winter, on snowy roads, we need to increase friction between the car tyres and the road surface. From the list below circle two ways in which this may be done.

    A) DRIVE MORE QUICKLY   **B) USE TYRES WITHOUT TREADS**

    C) DRIVE MORE SLOWLY   **D) USE GRIT ON ROADS**

The friction between a moving object and the air is called air resistance. Objects with low air resistance travel much easier than those with high air resistance.

Look at the 4 diagrams of vehicles and number them from 1 to 4. Number 1 will have the least air resistance and number 4 will have the most air resistance.

36 (____)   **37** (____)

38 (____)   **39** (____)

Complete the table about air resistance by ticking the correct box each time.

	OBJECT	HIGH AIR RESISTANCE	LOW AIR RESISTANCE
40	Formula One Racing Car		
41	A parachute being used		
42	A downhill ski-racer		
43	An oak leaf falling from a tree		

PHYSICAL PROCESSES PAGE 13

44 Four boys wanted to see if 2cm³ cubes of lead, wood, cork, and glass would float. Paul tried his experiment using ordinary water, Brian used a mixture of salt and water, Chris used oil and Philip used milk. Why was this not a fair test?

_____

Look at this table and answer the questions about it.

	Floats as a 1cm cube	Floats when saucer shaped
Lead	✗	✔
Plastic	✔	✔
Wood	✔	✔
Glass	✗	✔

45 List those things which sink when cube shaped? (_____)

46 List those things which float when cube shaped? (_____)

47 According to this table what helps to make things float? (_____)

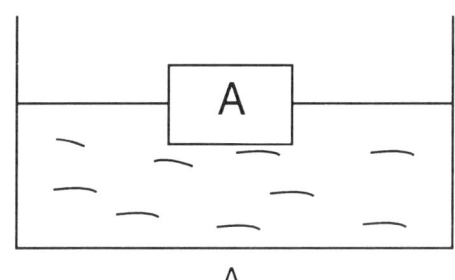
A

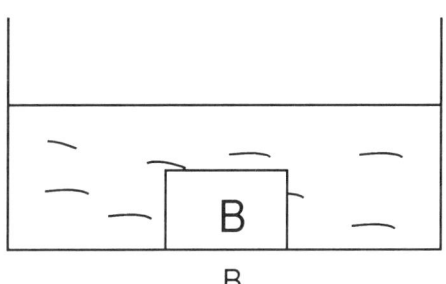
B

Look at the diagrams above of objects in dishes of water. Complete the statements below by circling words in the brackets.

48 In diagram A the force of gravity is (**greater than, less than, equal to**) the upward force of the water on the object.

49 In diagram B the force of gravity is (**greater than, less than, equal to**) the upward force of the water on the object.

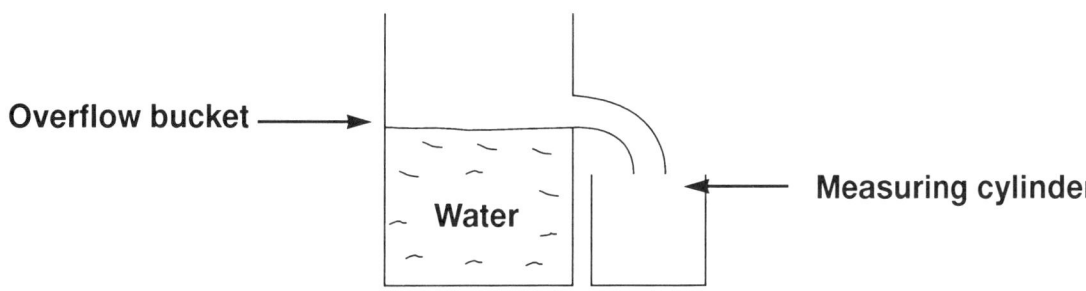

50 Look at this diagram of an overflow bucket. A cuboid of lead measuring 3 cm x 2 cm x 6 cm is placed into the water. How much water overflows into the measuring cylinder? (_____)

PHYSICAL PROCESSES PAGE 14

MATERIALS AND THEIR PROPERTIES TEST ONE

1) Yes, Yes, No
2) Yes, No, Yes
3) No, No, Yes
4) Brine, Mercury, Milk
5) Cork, Wood, Brass
6) Carbon dioxide, helium, oxygen
7) Sugar, salt
8 & 9) Natural - gold, cotton, milk
Man-made - glass, steel, plastic
10) Tin, lead, gold
11) Hydrogen, plastic, diamond
12) Water
13) b
14) Two variables instead of one (different materials & different locations)*
15) Opaque
16) Flexible
17) Shiny
18) Rough
19) Rigid
20) Transparent
21) Compass
22) Paper towels
23) Rubber Ball
24) Window Pane
25) Concrete Post
26) Rubber, wire
27) Coal, iron
28) Lead, glass, plastic, wood
29) a
30) P
31) T
32) T
33) P
34) P
35) P
36) Melts
37) Liquid
38) Evaporate
39) Gas
40) Solid
41) Liquid becomes gas
42) Solid becomes liquid
43) Liquid becomes solid
44) b & e
45) Oxygen
46) Carbon dioxide
47) c
48) Red
49) Red
50) Blue

* Or similar answer.

MATERIALS AND THEIR PROPERTIES TEST TWO

1 - 3) Liquid - mercury, oil
Solid - paper, sugar
Gas - hydrogen, oxygen
4 & 5) Manmade - nylon, polythene, cardboard
Natural - wood, leather, silver
6) c
7) a
8) c
9) Copper
10) Glass
11) Fibreglass
12) Concrete
13) Tissue paper
14) Rubber
15 & 16) b & f
17) b
18) Evaporate
19) Ignite
20) Melt
21) Condenses
22) Boil
23) Inflammable
24) Sun
25) Evaporate
26) Condenses
27) Clouds
28) Rain
29) Rivers
30) c
31) c
32) Oxygen
33) True
34) False
35) False
36) True
37) True
38) Milk
39) Sand (silica)
40) Trees (wood)
41) Clay
42) b & c
43) b & d
44 & 45) Moisture & oxygen (air)
46) C
47) B
48) A
49 & 50) Painting, galvanising, oiling etc.

ANSWERS PAGE 3

PHYSICAL PROCESSES TEST ONE

1) Gases
2) Solid
3) Earth
4) Star
5) Energy
6) Galaxy
7) Venus
8) Earth
9) Mars
10) Saturn
11) Uranus
12) Pluto
13) Rotation
14) Northern
15) Darkness
16) December
17) False
18) True
19) True
20) False
21) False
22) False
23) 30th June
24) 15th July
25) 5th August
26) 21st September
27) 29th November
28) 25th December
29) B
30) Tilt
31) Earth
32) Sun
33) Winter
34) Short
35) Long
36) Summer
37) Warmer
38) Autumn
39) Winter
40) Summer
41) Spring
42) B
43) B
44) C
45) Autumn
46) Winter
47) Summer
48) Winter
49) Spring
50) Winter

PHYSICAL PROCESSES TEST TWO

1) ✗
2) ✗
3) ✗
4) ✓
5) Anne
6) Jill
7) True
8) False
9) False
10) True
11) Attract
12) Repel
13) Repel
14) Attract
15) Magnetic field
16) D
17) A
18) D
19&20) Insulators - fork, cork, ball
Conductors - pipe, steel, foil
21) C
22) No
23) Yes
24) No
25) Yes
26) No
27) No
28) No
29) Yes
30&31) No battery, switch open
32) Yellow
33) Green
34) Blue
35) Backwards
36) Forwards
37) No direction
38) C
39&40) Pushing - Jet engines, bulldozer
Pulling - Car, tractor
41&42) Pushing - A, D, E
Pulling - B, C, F
43) Force
44) Centre
45) Surface
46) Space
47) Fall
48-50) B, E, F.

PHYSICAL PROCESSES TEST THREE

1) String
2) Air
3) Skin
4) E
5) D
6) Air
7&8) A, D
9) True
10) False
11) True
12) True
13) False
14) False
15) B
16-21) Potential - coal, food, battery, gas
Kinetic - river, wind
22&23) Read answers left to right
Effort, load, pivot
Effort, load, pivot
24) Twice
25) Clockwise
26&27) A - Clockwise
C - Anticlockwise
28) Parachute and air
29) Ice and skate
30) Blackboard and chalk
31) No
32) Yes
33) Yes
34) Yes
35) C & D
36) 4
37) 1
38) 2
39) 3
40) Low
41) High
42) Low
43) High
44) Two variables instead of one (different materials and different liquids)*
45) Lead, Glass
46) Wood, Plastic
47) Being saucer shaped
48) Equal to
49) Greater than
50) 36 cm^3

* Or similar answer.

LIFE PROCESSES & LIVING THINGS 2 TEST ONE

1) Spine / Backbone
2) I
3) V
4) V
5) V
6) I
7) I
8 - 13) With shell:- snail, crab, oyster
Without shell:- spider, butterfly jelly fish
14) Pupae
15) Adult fly
16) Eggs
17) Maggots
18) Pupae
19) Eggs
20) Maggots
21) Head
22) Thorax
23) Thorax
24) Abdomen
25) Head
26) Thorax
27) Crane fly
28) Beetle
29) Ant
30) Grasshopper
31) Mouth
32) Segment
33) Saddle
34) c
35) a
36) True
37) False
38) False
39) True
40) External
41) Molluscs
42) Protection
43) Slime
44) Tentacles
45) Eyes
46) 2
47) 8
48) Webs or silk
49) Predators
50) Insects

LIFE PROCESSES & LIVING THINGS 2 TEST TWO

1 - 8) Mammal - ape
Reptile - snake
Birds - sparrow, wren
Fish - cod, trout
Amphibians - newt, toad
9) Lays eggs *
10) Has gills *
11) Has scales and fins *
12) Scales
13) Dorsal fin
14) Tail fin
15) Gills
16 - 18) B, C, D
19) 5
20) 3
21) 2
22) 4
23) 6
24 - 26) a, d, e
27) Cold blooded
28) Temperature
29) Hot
30) Cold
31) Sunshine
32) F
33) T
34) F
35) T
36) T
37) ✓ ✓ ✗
38) ✓ ✗ ✗
39) ✗ ✗ ✓
40) ✓ ✗ ✓
41) ✓ ✗ ✗
42 - 44) Warm blooded **
Hair or fur, give birth to live young, suckle young.
45) F
46) F
47) T
48) F
49) T
50) F

* Any order.
** Any three.

LIFE PROCESSES & LIVING THINGS 2 TEST THREE

1) Yes
2) Yes
3) No
4) No
5) Yes
6) Yes
7 & 8) From plants - coal, paper
Not from plants - leather, silk
9) Bark
10) Flowers
11) Roots
12) Fruit
13) Stems
14) Leaves
15 & 16) c & f
17) 6 or all
18) Roots
19) Leaves
20) Flower
21) Fruits
22) Carbon dioxide
23) Oxygen
24 & 25) Flowering - daffodil & strawberry
Non-flowering - seaweed & moss
26) d
27) Stigma
28) Style
29) Anther
30) Stamen
31) Ovary
32) Sepal
33 & 34) Smell, colour
35 & 36) Animals, wind, humans*
37) The type of flower
38) Yes
39) No
40) Yes
41) Yes
42) No
43) No
44) b
45) 2
46) 4
47) 1
48) 3
49) 5
50) c

*Other answers possible.

ANSWERS

LIFE PROCESSES & LIVING THINGS 1 TEST ONE

1) Mandible or Jawbone
2) Femur or Thigh bone
3) Patella or Knee Cap
4 & 5) Skull / Brain
6 & 7) Ribs / Lungs or heart
8 & 9) Spine / Spinal cord
10) Ball and socket joint
11) Hinge joint
12) Gliding joint
13) Ball and socket joint
14) Pull
15 & 16) Contracts / Relaxes *
17) Push
18) Bob
19) c
20) b
21) 1
22) 4
23) 5
24) 2
25) 3
26) Running up sand dune
27) Sleeping
28) c
29) Right Atrium
30) Right Ventricle
31) Left Ventricle
32) Left Atrium
33) b, d
34) Arteries
35) Veins
36) Capillaries
37) Valves
38) Lungs
39) Kidneys
40) B
41) a, e
42) White Bread, Chicken Breast, Butter
43) a, c,
44) c, f
45) Molars
46) Canines
47) Incisors
48 - 50) Brush teeth regularly *
Eat fresh fruit and vegetables.
Avoid sugary foods /
visit dentist etc.

* Any order.

LIFE PROCESSES & LIVING THINGS 1 TEST TWO

1) Mouth
2) Oxygen
3) Carbon dioxide
4) Expelled
5) Diaphragm
6) True
7) True
8) False
9) True
10) Ventilation
11) Carbon dioxide
12) Oxygen
13) Less
14) Oxygen
15) b, d, e
16) Your nose helps warm the air going to your lungs. *
17) Hairs in your nose remove dust etc from the air. *
18) Peter
19) b
20) c
21) Mouth
22) Oesophagus
23) Stomach
24) Small Intestine
25) Large Intestine
26) Incisors
27) Canines
28) Molars / Premolars
29) Small Intestine
30) Mouth
31) Large Intestine
32) Stomach
33) True
34) True
35) True
36) False
37) True
38) True
39) quickly, large (or similar answers)
40) a, c, e
41) Mouth / Lips
42) Plastic tube
43) Lungs
44) It will fill with smoke and tar.
45) By pipe, cigar, etc.
46) E
47) D
48) B
49) A
50) C

* Any order.